COVERT CAREERS
Jobs You Can't Talk About

INSIDE THE
SECRET
SERVICE

LOUISE SPILSBURY

LUCENT
PRESS

Published in 2019 by
Lucent Press, an Imprint of Greenhaven Publishing, LLC
353 3rd Avenue
Suite 255
New York, NY 10010

Produced for Lucent by Calcium
Designers: Paul Myerscough and Jeni Child
Picture researcher: Rachel Blount
Editors: Sarah Eason and Jennifer Sanderson

Picture credits: Cover: Shutterstock: Daxiao Productions; Inside: Flickr: Elvert Barnes (CC
BY-SA 2.0): pp. 18, 19, 21tr; Shutterstock: Jai Agnish: p. 13; anaglic: p. 35; Andrey Popov:
p. 38; Couperfield: pp. 3, 28; Everett Historical: p. 7; KellyNelson: pp. 44–45t; Lightboxx:
p. 33; Pefostudio5: p. 29; Rawpixel.com: p. 36; mark reinstein: pp. 11, 23, 31; Sirtravelalot:
p. 41; TechWizard: p. 40; Roman Tiraspolsky: p. 4; Christian Vinces: p. 32; VP Photo Studio:
p. 17; Wavebreakmedia: p. 37; U.S. Air Force: Margo Wright: p. 25; U.S. Department of Homeland
Security: Pete Souza/U.S. Secret Service: p. 10; Wikimedia Commons: Official White House Photo
by Shealah Craighead: p. 26; Official DHS photo by Jetta Disco: p. 8; DoD photo by Zane Ecklund:
p. 27; Zane P Ecklund: p. 5; Glenn Fawcett: p. 16; Pete Souza: p. 42; The Bureau of Engraving and
Printing: p. 6; U.S. Department of State: p. 34; U.S. Secret Service: pp. 9, 12, 14, 15, 22, 24, 39, 43;
White House Photographic Collection: p. 30; Erik Winblad: pp. 20–21b.

Cataloging-in-Publication Data

Names: Spilsbury, Louise.
Title: Inside the Secret Service / Louise Spilsbury.
Description: New York : Lucent Press, 2019. | Series: Covert careers: jobs you can't talk about |
Includes glossary and index.
Identifiers: ISBN 9781534566354 (pbk.) | ISBN 9781534566361 (library bound) |
ISBN 9781534566378 (ebook)
Subjects: LCSH: Secret service--United States--Juvenile literature.
Classification: LCC HV8144.S43 S65 2019 | DDC 363.28'30973--dc23

Printed in the United States of America

CPSIA compliance information: Batch BW19KL: For further information, contact Greenhaven
Publishing, LLC, New York, New York, at 1-844-317-7404.

Please visit our website, www.greenhavenpublishing.com. For a free color catalog of all our
high-quality books, call toll free 1-844-317-7404 or fax 1-844-317-7405.

CONTENTS

CHAPTER 1

WHAT IS THE SECRET SERVICE?

The Secret Service is one of the oldest federal investigative law enforcement agencies in the United States. Secret Service agents are the men and women whose job it is to guard the president of the United States and other powerful and important people. These agents are also tasked with investigating and preventing illegal activities, such as major financial crimes, against the United States.

Protection Professionals

Secret Service agents investigate potential threats, make plans to keep the president safe at events, and guard the president when he attends events. As well as the president and his family, by law, the Secret Service is also authorized to protect:

- The U.S. vice president, the president-elect, vice president-elect, and their families
- Former U.S. presidents and their immediate families
- Visiting leaders of foreign states or governments and their spouses traveling with them, other important foreign visitors to the United States, and official representatives of the United States performing special missions overseas
- Presidential and vice presidential candidates and their partners within 120 days of a presidential election
- Other individuals as designated per executive order of the president

Secret Service agents are trained to investigate and protect.

Whenever and wherever you see the president of the United States, you will see Secret Service agents.

Other Important Duties

The Secret Service also investigates criminal cases that are related to the nation's financial security. It safeguards the financial systems of the United States from a wide range of financial and computer-based crimes, such as the making of counterfeit U.S. currency, the forgery or theft of U.S. Treasury checks and bonds, credit card fraud, identity theft, and certain other crimes. Secret Service agents and officers also take the lead in security operations at major events, such as the Super Bowl.

Inside the Secret Service

The Secret Service does not hire many people, so anyone who wants to join this respected organization will have to be incredibly determined to do so. The Secret Service has a strict and lengthy application process, which includes several rounds of interviews and thorough background checks. Those who successfully make it through then face a demanding and grueling training regime.

History of the Secret Service

The Secret Service was founded on July 5, 1865, after the end of the Civil War. President Abraham Lincoln originally created the Secret Service to investigate and stop the counterfeiting of U.S. currency, which was a problem at that time. In fact, it was estimated that immediately following the Civil War, one-third to one-half of all the money in circulation in the United States was fake. The Secret Service was set up as a branch of the U.S. Treasury Department, and William P. Wood was made the division's first Chief, a role now known as Director. In 1867, the role of the agency was expanded to include investigations of mail theft, bootlegging (the illegal manufacturing and selling of alcohol), smuggling, and fraud.

The creation of the Secret Service was one of the last acts that Abraham Lincoln signed. Later that evening, he was assassinated.

A Mission to Protect

In 1901, President William McKinley was shot and critically wounded during an event in Buffalo, New York. McKinley died eight days later and became the third sitting U.S. president to be assassinated. After McKinley's death, Vice President Theodore Roosevelt was sworn into office. McKinley's assassination prompted Congress to request full-time Secret Service protection for Roosevelt and all future presidents. In 1902, the Secret Service sent two men to the White House to protect the president 24 hours a day, 7 days a week.

Growing and Changing

Gradually, the U.S. Secret Service grew from a small department with just a few staff to a major organization. There were other changes along the way:

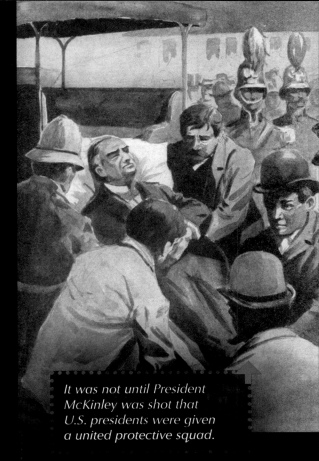

It was not until President McKinley was shot that U.S. presidents were given a united protective squad.

✔ 1930: The White House police force became part of the Secret Service, now known as the Uniformed Division.
✔ 1936: Operatives became known as agents.
✔ 1953: The first formal special service training school for agents opened.
✔ 1970: Phyllis Shantz became the first female officer.
✔ 1971: The James T. Rowley Training Center for Secret Service agents was established.
✔ 1999: The Secret Service headquarters opened in Washington, D.C.
✔ 2001: A network of Electronic Crimes Task Forces was set up to prevent, detect, and investigate electronic crimes.
✔ 2003: The Secret Service moved from the Treasury Department to the Department of Homeland Security.
✔ 2012: A law was passed giving presidents protection for life.
✔ 2013: Julia Pierson became the first female director of the Secret Service.

Investigate and Protect

Today, the U.S. Secret Service is a law enforcement organization of nearly 7,000 employees worldwide. It continues to protect both presidents and visiting world leaders while also leading financial and cybercrime investigations. From its headquarters, a nine-story brick building in Washington, D.C., it runs field offices located in the United States, Canada, Mexico, and countries in South America, Europe, Africa, and Asia, working with law enforcement organizations in those areas when necessary.

This is a meeting of Secret Service employees, the Secretary of Homeland Security, and the Director of the Secret Service at its headquarters.

Secret Service Agents

The public face of the Secret Service is its agents. These are the men and women seen wearing suits and dark glasses running alongside the president's motorcade or guarding the president's family as it attends a public event. Secret Service agents have the power to make arrests and must be ready to grab their gun or wrestle a suspicious individual to the ground in a moment. However, Secret Service agents also rely on a team of other Secret Service officers and workers who provide the tools and technology, physical support, and intelligence, without which the agents could not complete their missions.

The Commission Book

All Secret Service agents carry a commission book, which looks like a small wallet. Inside, it contains a badge with the Secret Service star, a photo identification (ID), and credentials to prove that the agent is who they say they are. It affirms that they are, by law, allowed to carry firearms, make arrests, and protect the president. On the back is the Secret Service official motto: "Worthy of Trust and Confidence."

The Secret Service Shield

Secret Service agents and officers are proud to carry the agency's badge as a symbol of the duties and responsibilities they are entrusted to perform. The badge is small enough for agents to easily carry it in their commission books. The star's five points each represent one of the agency's five core values: justice, duty, courage, honesty, and loyalty.

The Secret Service badge instills great pride in the agents who carry it.

THE SECRET SERVICE IN ACTION

The Secret Service organization has two main priorities: protection and investigation. Secret Service agents and officers protect the president and other important people. They protect places and provide security and protection at important events. They also investigate serious financial crimes.

Protecting the President

Protecting the president is a challenging and sometimes dangerous job. Danger can come at the president from any direction. He might become a target for a lone shooter in a crowd or a major terrorist attack, such as a bombing. Agents who work for the Presidential Protective Division, or PPD, are usually selected from a small group of people who have proven themselves over the years. The presidential protection job can look rather glamorous, since some agents fly all over the world, but it can be a difficult job. Agents are trained to take a bullet, and some have even lost their lives in order to save a president.

Secret Service agents on presidential protection duty may work two weeks on a day shift, followed by two weeks on a midnight shift, then two weeks on an evening shift, followed by two weeks of training.

President Bill Clinton regularly went jogging when he was in office, so his agents had to do the same!

Protection Details

Those people who are permanently protected, such as the president and his wife, have groups of agents assigned to them. These groups of agents are known as "details." The details that are assigned to physically protect the president go everywhere with him, even to doctor's appointments and the restroom. The agents have to do what the president does. So if, for example, the president rides horses or goes jogging for exercise, the agents in his detail must ride or run beside him. When the president is eating away from the White House, some agents watch the president's meal being prepared to make sure no one tries to poison it.

Inside the Secret Service

Secret Service agents keep the president and other important people safe all the time, every day. It is not a 9-to-5 job, so Secret Service agents must be prepared to work anywhere and at any time.

Homeland Security

Since 1998, events that require protection by the Secret Service have been known as National Special Security Events. They are events of national or international importance that the United States Department of Homeland Security believe to be potential targets for terrorism or other criminal activity. These events include meetings between heads of world governments, such as G20 and United Nations summits, and presidential conventions, president-elect pre-inauguration train tours, and inaugurations.

The G20 Summit

The G20 is a group of heads of state or government from the world's 20 largest economic powers. The G20 meets to discuss financial markets and the world economy. The G20 meeting in 2009 was held in Pittsburgh, Pennsylvania. It was designated a National Special Security Event by Homeland Security.

The Secret Service is famous for the physical protection it provides to U.S. and other world leaders.

The Secret Service was put in charge of providing protection for heads of state. It worked alongside local law enforcement officials enforcement agencies, such as the Federal Bureau of Investigat Service divided up the work to deal with specific security conce protection, waterways, airspace, intelligence gathering, training and getting information to the media and the public.

Security at the Super Bowl

At all the National Special Security Events, the Secret Service c other law enforcement agencies to keep people and places safe security operation such as the Super Bowl, the Secret Service is agencies that work together. One of the tasks the Secret Service for is combing through messages on social media platforms, su Facebook, to discover clues to any possible terror threats. The S helps improve cybersecurity to protect systems, networks, and c Bowl. It also trains security personnel to use magnetometers at

Inside the Secret Service

Secret Service agents and officers regularly work alongside other law enforcement agencies, so they must be able to cooperate and get along with a wide range of people. Their lives and the lives of others depend on it.

Investigating Crimes

When the Secret Service first started investigating financial crimes in the nineteenth century, its work mainly consisted of tracking down and arresting the people who were printing fake U.S. bills. Today, Secret Service agents and officers have to investigate and stop far more complicated forms of financial Internet or computer crimes, including:

These Secret Service agents are investigating crimes as part of the Financial Crimes Task Force.

✔ Phishing emails: emails that trick people into clicking on a link that enables criminals to get sensitive information, such as usernames, passwords, and credit card information, from their computers

✔ Account takeovers: when company or personal accounts—including bank accounts, credit cards, email, and other service provider accounts—are taken over by fraudsters

✔ Malware: malicious software that brings harm to a computer system in the form of worms, viruses, Trojan horses, and spyware, which steal protected data, delete documents, or add software not approved by a user

✔ Hacking: unauthorized entry into a computer or network of computers to steal information or data

Investigation Techniques

Trained Secret Service analysts in electronic and financial crimes task forces gather data and look for patterns in credit card theft, identity theft, money laundering, and other crimes. The agency also has an advanced forensics lab. This contains an ink library that holds thousands of samples that can be used to identify or date various documents related to a crime that is being investigated. There is also a handwriting database, which has digitized copies of handwriting found, for example, in threatening letters. These handwriting samples can be quickly compared to other samples to link criminals to crimes. The agency also has access to databases for matching fingerprints, matching pharmaceutical drugs, analyzing the tread patterns made by different shoes, and analyzing bullet and cartridge casings.

Successful Investigations

In the Secret Service annual report for 2016, the agency made more than 251 cybercrime arrests, preventing $558 million in potential loss and $125 million in actual loss. It also kept more than $64 million in counterfeit U.S. currency from being circulated. More than 2,100 arrests were made, as well as more than 238 seizures of counterfeit money, which resulted in the recovery of $46 million.

This Secret Service analyst is examining counterfeit documents.

CHAPTER 3

THE SECRET SERVICE TEAM

Special agents may be the Secret Service workers that are most familiar, but the Secret Service team is made up of a variety of career positions. The Secret Service has challenging and complex jobs and missions, so it requires the help of a wide range of individuals and talents.

Vital Background Work

Administration workers and professionals help run the organization. For example, support assistants run an agent's office, open and maintain case files, process and track evidence, and provide the necessary administrative support for a special agent's investigations. Attorney advisers give legal advice and assistance on a wide range of matters. Accountants look after the organization's finances. Writer-editors prepare scripts, written materials, speeches for the director, and things such as news releases, pamphlets, and brochures. Protective support technicians maintain and organize the security vehicles, such as armored cars, that are used in Secret Service operations.

President Trump appointed Randolph D. Alles as the 25th Director of the Secret Service on April 25, 2017.

Making Missions Happen

There are many jobs that are more directly involved in Secret Service investigations and missions. Many of these jobs involve extensive practical knowledge and are often quite technical. For example:

There is a huge variety of jobs at the Secret Service, requiring many different skills.

- Document analysts use scientific techniques to analyze things such as handwriting, credit cards, inks, and paper to identify documents that can be used as evidence in criminal investigations.
- Fingerprint specialists are skilled at finding and enhancing latent fingerprints on any surface and carrying out automated fingerprint ID searches to link suspects to crime scenes.
- Physical security specialists conduct surveys of sites to identify what security will be needed. They set up systems for detection and surveillance at protected sites.
- Investigative analysts analyze information about people suspected of posing a threat to Secret Service protectees and provide intelligence to help agents protect people.
- Criminal research specialists use computer programs to track and analyze investigations and liaise with other law enforcement agencies when investigating financial crimes.

Inside the Secret Service

People working in administrative, professional, and technical (APT) jobs do valuable work at the Secret Service. They usually work in an office or laboratory, but they may also travel to meetings or court hearings. Many have a college education or specialized training, although some positions are also gained through on-the-job experience.

Uniformed Division Officers

The special badge worn by uniformed officers represents their **major** area of responsibility: the White House. Officers in the Uniformed Division are those who protect the White House complex and the vice president's residence at the Naval Observatory. They also provide security for the Treasury Department building and foreign diplomatic missions in Washington, D.C.

Uniformed Officers at Work

The men and women of the Uniformed Division work alongside Secret Service agents on White House security arrangements. Some members of the Uniformed Division patrol the White House grounds by car, on foot, or on bicycle. They monitor the grounds and buildings, and check that security equipment, such as surveillance cameras, is working correctly. They also patrol and monitor the streets and parks near the White House, with help from Washington police officers. Uniformed officers are authorized to stop, search, question, and arrest anyone who trespasses on White House grounds or behaves in a disruptive or potentially dangerous way.

Secret Service Uniformed Division officers wear uniforms so they can be recognized as police officers.

Officers of the Secret Service are constantly on the watch for any disturbances or suspicious or criminal activity.

Standing Guard

Some uniformed officers stand guard in fixed positions—for example, at entrances to the White House. They also stand guard at checkpoints, stopping and checking vehicles entering the White House to be sure they are not carrying explosives or weapons. Other uniformed officers operate magnetometers at the White House and other sites to prevent people from taking items such as firearms into buildings. Unlike regular Secret Service agents, uniformed officers regularly chat with tourists who visit the White House.

Protecting the White House

White House vehicle entrances are highly protected with heavy barricades that only open to let one vehicle through at a time. If anyone tries to jump over the fence or cross any of the barriers, the White House goes into immediate lockdown. No one is allowed to enter or leave the White House grounds until the emergency has been investigated and is under control.

Specialized Units

After some years of experience, the most exceptional officers in the Secret Service may be selected to join one of several specialized units. The specialized units include:

✔ Canine Unit: These agents use sniffer dogs to check for and respond to bomb threats and suspicious packages.

✔ Emergency Response Team: This team is ready to use firearms in the event of any attack on the White House and other protected facilities.

✔ Countersniper Team: These highly trained sharpshooters use specially designed sniper rifles to stop anyone who threatens protectees.

✔ Motorcade Support Unit: These officers ride motorcycles alongside motorcades.

✔ Crime Scene Search Unit: This unit photographs, collects, and processes evidence at crime scenes.

✔ Office of Training: These officers serve as firearms and classroom instructors, or recruiters.

✔ Special Operations Section: This division handles special duties and functions at the White House complex, such as conducting tours of the White House.

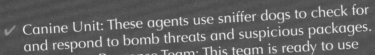

Secret Service snipers assume rooftop positions along the route that the presidential motorcade travels.

Special Officers

The Secret Service also has a Special Officers division. Special officers perform a wide range of security duties, and they support protective assignments. They may maintain security posts, inspect protective vehicles to ensure they are fit for their purpose, or drive or follow protective vehicles closely in a motorcade. They help control who is allowed into Secret Service facilities, and they monitor and operate communications equipment and technologies that detect high-risk items, such as firearms, at entrances to those facilities. Special officers are authorized to stop and arrest suspects.

Some Secret Service officers ride motorcycles alongside the presidential motorcade.

Inside the Secret Service

Many Secret Service officers do advance work to assess threat levels in order to prevent an incident from occurring. For example, when the president travels, every hotel employee may be subjected to a background check. If any staff member has even a minor criminal record, that person will be banned from work during the president's visit. This kind of screening requires a great deal of patience, an eye for detail, and persistence.

Finding clues that solve crimes is just one part of a Secret Service agent's job.

Special Agents

Being a special agent is one of the most exciting careers in the Secret Service. Special agents carry out assignments in both protection and investigation missions, but primarily, special agents are criminal investigators. They investigate violations of laws relating to financial crimes such as credit card and access device fraud, as well as computer-based attacks on U.S. banking and telecommunications institutions. They may, for example, be in the field conducting a search on a counterfeit case or in the office scanning through surveillance images of criminals suspected of using credit cards stolen from the postal services. They might collect handwriting samples or fingerprints and send them to the Secret Service forensic lab to see if the evidence can be used to link a criminal to a case. When they get the evidence they need, they arrest the criminal in question.

A Demanding Job

Special agents who protect the president or other high-level officials have a demanding job. They may have to stay awake for 24 hours, skip meals, stand outside a house in the rain at night, and board a plane for a long flight. They might be called to an assignment at short notice and miss holidays, birthdays, and other life events that matter to them. Some agents working close to the president and traveling alongside him on foreign visits can be away from home for 30 days at a time and even up to a total of eight months of the year.

Secret Service agents have the right to make arrests during an investigation.

Curious Code Names

The United States Secret Service uses code names for the locations and people it protects. Before communications could be encrypted for safety, code names were used for security. Today, they are used more for brevity and clarity. Code names include "Rawhide" for Ronald Reagan, "Renegade" for Barack Obama, and "Mogul" for Donald Trump. Agents call the Pentagon "Calico" and refer to the White House as "Castle."

TECHNIQUES AND TOOLS

The Secret Service uses an array of gadgets to help agents and officers do their jobs. Some of the technology and tools they use seem simple, but they are actually very important.

Agent Outfits

For protective and investigative assignments, agents use their standard-issue weapons and handcuffs, and a radio to maintain contact with each other. They also are issued with bullet-resistant vests. These vests are worn over the torso and fit under a shirt and jacket. They help absorb, or reduce, the impact and keep bullets or shrapnel from explosions from penetrating the body. Secret Service agents sometimes wear reflective sunglasses to keep the sun out of their eyes. Sunglasses also make it easier to see what people in the crowd are doing, without individuals knowing that the agent is looking at them. Sunglasses also deflect any liquids or objects that people might throw at them.

Secret Service agents wear sunglasses to keep the sun out of their eyes. This helps them see what people in a crowd are doing.

Agent Earpieces

Secret Service agents are often shown talking into their sleeves. Each agent wears a small microphone just inside their sleeve, so that they can speak into it easily while keeping their hands free to hold a weapon, if necessary. They speak into the microphone next to their wrist, and they hear replies through an earpiece. This allows them to communicate with other Secret Service agents and officers, so that they can keep each other informed about where the president is at all times. The communications system is also linked to a special command center that gives agents in the field directions and tells them all the information they need to complete a mission.

Before going on duty, agents wear an earpiece, so that they know where the president is at all times.

Canine Capers

The Secret Service uses dogs from the Netherlands called Belgian Malinois to detect explosives, drugs, and firearms as part of the K-9 division. These short-haired dogs adapt well to new climates and environments and work very hard for their specially trained handlers. The dogs are also trained to attack intruders to the White House. They can run 30 miles (50 km) per hour and have a bite that applies hundreds of pounds of pressure per square inch.

Secrets of the Oval Office

To maintain the president's privacy, Secret Service agents do not stand inside the Oval Office. They stand guard outside its doors instead. When the doors are closed, agents still know what the president is doing because there are weight-sensitive pressure pads under the carpet. These let the agents know exactly where the president is at all times. A retired Secret Service agent also revealed that some of the ornaments bearing the presidential seal inside the Oval Office are actually secret alarms. He said that all a president has to do is turn one over, and Secret Service agents will come running.

The president's Oval Office is fitted with sensors and alarms to keep the president safe at all times, even when out of sight of Secret Service agents.

The Beast

"The Beast" is the nickname for the president's custom-built Cadillac limousine. This car weighs around 15,000 to 20,000 pounds (6,800 to 9,071 kg) and costs an estimated $1.5 million. The Secret Service is believed to keep about 12 copies of the vehicle. The Beast is outfitted with many offensive and defensive measures:

- ✔ Each of the doors is 8 inches (20 cm) thick and completely seals the cabin to prevent chemical or biological attacks.
- ✔ The windows are made of 5-inch- (13 cm) thick bulletproof glass.
- ✔ It has bulletproof tires, and the body has armor plating and is both bulletproof and bombproof.
- ✔ The fuel tank is armor-plated and covered in special foam to keep it from being damaged in a collision or by bullets.
- ✔ Its bodywork is made from a variety of strong materials, including steel, aluminum, titanium, and ceramics.
- ✔ It is equipped with night vision cameras, GPS tracking, and a satellite communication system to allow it to drive in any conditions and so that the president can always be contacted.
- ✔ It has a supply of oxygen and emergency medical equipment, including bottles of blood that are the president's blood type, in case the ambulance that travels in the motorcade is cut off.

The president's official vehicle, a custom-built Cadillac limousine, is as heavy as a tank and is equipped with several protection features.

Inside the Secret Service

Agents that drive the president's limousine or any of the vehicles in the motorcade have to have extensive experience in defensive driving. They have to be able to drive very quickly—and yet, very safely—away from a dangerous situation without any hesitation.

The Secret Service has a variety of technologies that help it investigate crimes and analyze evidence. For example:

- ✔ A high-powered microscope is used by investigators to verify the printing method used to create a collection of counterfeit notes.
- ✔ An ultraviolet (UV) light source can be used to check if bills are real or fake.
- ✔ Forensic scientists use state-of-the-art techniques to enhance audio and video recordings to assist field investigators.
- ✔ A voice identification program can be used to identify a person from the characteristics of their voice, including pronunciation, emphasis, speed of speech, and accent, as well as the effects of physical elements, such as the shape and size of the mouth and nasal passage.

UV light can be used to reveal forensic evidence, such as fingerprints.

DNA Collector

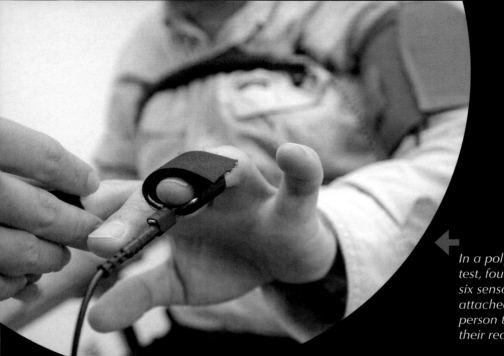

In a polygraph test, four to six sensors are attached to a person to record their reactions.

Polygraph Tests

The Secret Service uses a polygraph, or lie detector, to determine whether a person they are investigating and questioning is telling the truth. Polygraphs work by sensing and measuring how someone's body reacts when they are asked a question. Once the suspect is attached to the polygraph, a Secret Service examiner starts by asking simple questions that can be answered only with a "yes" or a "no," such as, "Are you 100 years old?" and then more subtle questions, such as "Have you ever lied to someone who trusts you?" The machine measures the suspect's blood pressure, pulse (the number of times a minute their heart beats), the amount they sweat, and the rate at which they respire, or breathe. By analyzing the results, the examiner can judge whether or not the suspect is telling the truth.

Finding Fingerprints

Fingerprints are the perfect way to link a criminal to a crime because everyone's fingerprints are unique. The conventional method of getting prints was to dust black powder on them and lift the powder on a sticky sheet. Now, forensic photographers use special kinds of light to make it possible to see fingerprints on evidence that previously would have been invisible.

CHAPTER 5

FAMOUS SECRET SERVICE CASES

The men and women of the Secret Service have been involved in some very important missions. They have saved presidents' lives, protected leaders from all around the world, and put the ringleaders of some major financial crime syndicates behind bars.

An Attempted Assassination

On Monday, March 30, 1981, a lone gunman attempted to assassinate the then president, Ronald Reagan. John Hinckley Jr. had a history of mental health problems and planned to shoot the president as part of a misguided scheme to attract the attention of actress Jodie Foster, with whom he had become obsessed. Reagan was addressing a conference at the Washington Hilton hotel, so Hinckley waited outside the hotel for Reagan to leave. He fired six shots, injuring the president, a Secret Service agent, a police officer, and a press officer.

This photograph was taken moments before President Reagan was shot in 1981. After being shot, President Reagan had several hours of surgery but eventually made a complete recovery.

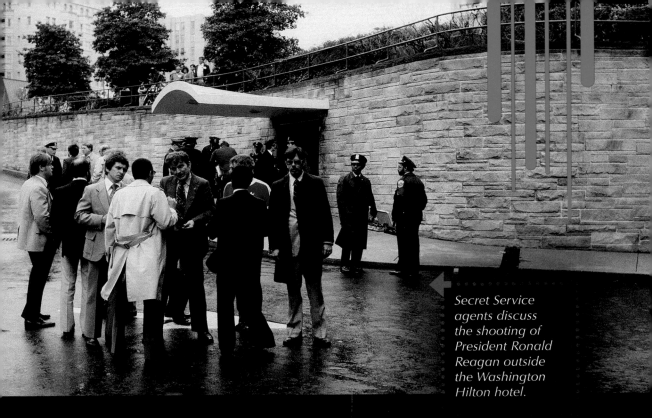

Secret Service agents discuss the shooting of President Ronald Reagan outside the Washington Hilton hotel.

Saving President Reagan

Agent Jerry Parr was in charge of President Reagan's detail that day. As soon as the shots were fired, Parr sprang into action. He pushed the president inside his limousine and ordered the driver to speed to the White House. As the limousine drove off, Parr checked Reagan's body. He could not see any bullet wounds, and both Parr and Reagan thought the pain felt by the president in his chest was likely just a rib injury. However, Parr then noticed frothy red blood coming from Reagan's lips. This was an indication that the president was bleeding from the lungs—a dangerous and life-threatening condition. Parr immediately ordered the limousine to be driven to George Washington Hospital. Doctors there confirmed that Reagan had been shot in the lung and was suffering from internal bleeding. If Parr had not acted so quickly, President Reagan would certainly have died.

Inside the Secret Service

Protecting the president is a huge responsibility. Secret Service agents who do this job know that their split-second decisions could make the difference between a president's life and death. One wrong choice could haunt them forever.

The Secret Service mission known as Operation Sunset was run from an office in Lima, Peru.

Operation Sunset

Operation Sunset was a major Secret Service anti-counterfeit currency operation in Peru. Peru is the world's largest manufacturer and distributor of counterfeit U.S. currency, so the U.S. Secret Service opened a Resident Office in Lima, the capital city of Peru. From here, the Secret Service increased its efforts to stop the widespread counterfeit activity by setting up an anti-Counterfeiting Task Force. The Secret Service began training Peruvian National Police officers at Secret Service training facilities.

Agents at Work

The Task Force worked alongside Peruvian police officers to gather intelligence. They focused their investigations on six Peruvian-based criminal organizations. It was a challenging task. In the United States and much of Europe, the Secret Service and other law enforcement agencies closely monitor the sale, distribution, and use of offset printers, which are used to print fake money. However, in Peru, anyone can buy an offset printer without being checked, and entire neighborhoods make and sell all kinds of fake documents and currencies.

After careful investigations lasting more than two years, Secret Service agents and Peruvian police had enough evidence to order search and arrest warrants on a counterfeiting ring in Lima. Just before dawn on November 15, 2016, the raid began. The facts and figures of the raid are impressive:

- ✓ More than 1,500 Peruvian National Police officers were involved in the operation.
- ✓ A total of 54 search warrants were conducted, and 48 people were arrested.
- ✓ Thirty million counterfeit U.S. dollars and 50,000 euros were discovered.
- ✓ Six counterfeit plants were seized, as well as eight counterfeit manufacturing presses and more than 1,600 printing plates and negatives of bills of varying values.

The Secrets of Smuggling

Every month, millions of fake bills are smuggled out of Peru and into the United States by couriers known as burriers. The burriers travel by airplane to Mexico and hide the counterfeit cash in creative ways, such as inside children's toys, hollowed-out books, the soles of sneakers, or picture frames. From Mexico, the fake money is smuggled over the border into the United States.

Operation Sunset was the largest raid of counterfeit currency in the Secret Service's history.

The United Nations (UN) is home to the UN Security Council, the body responsible for world security and peace. Each year, the leaders on the Council come together to discuss the world's most complex problems at the UN General Assembly. The Secret Service is in charge of safety at these summits. The summits are particularly challenging because many foreign leaders stay in the same hotels and attend the same events at the same times each year, giving criminals plenty of time to plan an attack. Security for the 2017 UN General Assembly was especially rigorous.

Teamwork

The Secret Service worked with thousands of New York City police officers to secure buildings and traffic routes, and lead motorcades. Traffic congestion posed the risk of motorcades being slowed down and becoming possible targets for an ambush, so Secret Service agents and police officers stood guard while concrete and steel barricades blocked streets around the UN buildings. Protesters marched near the buildings while the summit was taking place, so to limit any risk, the Secret Service also made sure that pedestrians were kept well back during the General Assembly.

Secret Service agents protect world leaders in and around the UN Headquarters Building in New York City.

Protecting Foreign Leaders

The Secret Service ran the security arrangements from operation centers. Agents were assigned to individual world leaders and tasked with protecting their life and getting them safely from one place to another for six days, from airports to hotels to meetings. Fleets of black cars ferried world leaders around, and all vehicles coming to the UN building were inspected before they were allowed to enter the UN garage to drop off delegates. Secret Service officers and agents were posted on rooftops to keep surveillance of the area, so that they could spot any suspicious activity.

This notice on a streetlight informs people of security zone road closures before a UN General Assembly summit.

United Nations General Assembly
NO STOPPING ANYTIME
24 HOURS A DAY
SECURITY ZONE
VEHICLES SUBJECT TO TOW
BY ORDER OF
THE DEPARTMENT CITY OF NEW YORK

Inside the Secret Service

Secret Service agents must protect anyone to whom they are assigned. In the case of the UN summit, that may sometimes include world leaders who are enemies of the United States. The agents must still do their job to the very best of their ability, even if their protectee makes them somewhat uncomfortable.

CHAPTER 6

A COVERT CAREER

The agents who work for the Secret Service are very proud of their role in keeping their nation safe. Thousands of people apply to the Secret Service each year, but only a couple hundred are hired. How do men and women succeed in this covert career?

Starting Off

People who want to become Secret Service agents should study hard in all subjects at school. This will help them learn the variety of skills that agents use every day, such as: science, computer science, law and government, arithmetic, reading comprehension, writing, foreign languages, and public speaking. Most applicants also have a four-year college degree or a combination of education and criminal investigative experience.

Applicants must medically remove body markings such as tattoos before applying for a job with the Secret Service.

esearch

nyone applying to the Secret Service should also do their search and learn about the agency before applying to join e training program. Secret Service interviewers might, for ample, ask applicants what they know about the different visions of the Service or what they know about the duties Secret Service agents. It is best to be prepared.

Secret Service physical training is tough, so applicants must be physically fit.

be considered for positions, an applicant must:

- ✔ Be a U.S. citizen
- ✔ Be between 21 and 37 years of age
- ✔ Have a current valid driver's license
- ✔ Have good eyesight
- ✔ Be in excellent health and physical condition
- ✔ Pass a written examination
- ✔ Pass a physical fitness test
- ✔ Qualify for security clearance and undergo a complete background check, including interviews, being tested for drugs, and medical and polygraph examinations
- ✔ Have no visible body markings (such as tattoos, body art, and branding) on the head, face, neck, hand, and fingers (any area below the wrist bone)

Inside the Secret Service

All applicants to the Secret Service must pass the Secret Service Applicant Physical Abilities Test (APAT). Physical fitness tests check that trainees are fit for training and duty. The fitness evaluation measures strength, endurance, and aerobic capacity using four main challenges: push-ups, sit-ups, chin-ups, and the 1.5-mile (2.4 km) run.

Time for Training?

It can take up to a year to be accepted onto a Secret Service training program. This is because everyone in the Secret Service has to have a top-secret security clearance, and it can take six to nine months to complete a thorough background check on an applicant to get this. The investigation checks all the background details of an applicant's life, such as their educational qualifications and employment history, their vehicle license and police records, their financial history, and military records.

Criminal Investigator Training Program

After an applicant is accepted onto the new agent training program, their first stop is the Federal Law Enforcement Training Center (FLETC) in Glynco, Georgia. Here, they take part in the Criminal Investigator Training Program (CITP). This 56-day course includes lectures, laboratory activities, practical exercises, and written exams in areas such as criminal law and investigative techniques. Throughout the program, trainees work in small teams doing an investigation to learn skills such as how to interview witnesses, how to do surveillance and undercover operations, and how to write and execute search and arrest warrants, write a criminal complaint, and give evidence in a courtroom hearing.

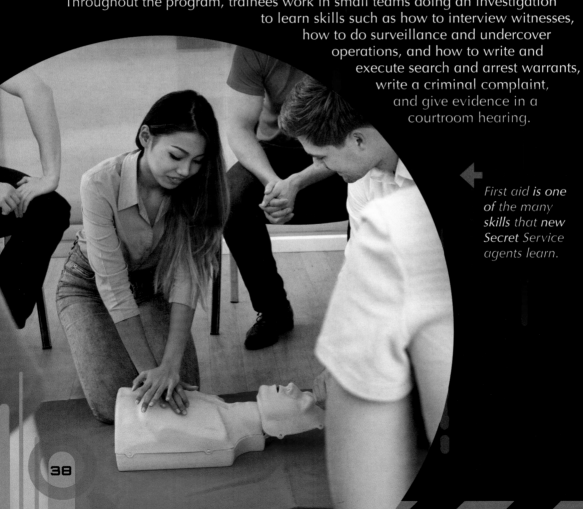

First aid is one of the many skills that new Secret Service agents learn.

Special Agent Training Course

f they successfully complete the CITP course, new agent trainees do the 17-week Special Agent Training Course at the James J. Rowley Training Center (JJRTC, RTC, or Secret Service Academy). This course focuses on the basic knowledge and advanced skills needed for the Secret Service's dual responsibilities of investigations and protection. Trainees learn about:

Trainee agents learn to use scanners to keep government buildings secure.

- ✓ Combating counterfeiting, fraud, and other financial criminal activity
- ✓ Investigating people who are a potential threat to the United States
- ✓ Physical security techniques, such as surveillance
- ✓ How to do a security survey of a future trip, to include hotels, restaurants, vehicles, other transportation, hospitals, doctors, and routes of travel
- ✓ Emergency medical skills

Becoming a Uniformed Division Officer

Trainee Secret Service Uniformed Division officers do the same 56-day Criminal Investigator Training Program (CITP) as trainee agents. Then, they do 12 weeks of specialized training, which includes classroom study and on-the-job experience. They learn a variety of skills, including police procedures, handling firearms, physical fitness, psychology, police-community relations, criminal law, first aid, laws of arrest, search and seizure, physical defense techniques, and international treaties.

The James J. Rowley Training Center

During the Special Agent Training Course, trainees also have extensive training in skills such as marksmanship, tactics to disarm and control suspects, and dealing with other dangerous situations they might find themselves in. The James J. Rowley Training Center is just outside Washington, D.C, in Laurel, Maryland, and is unmarked and hidden behind barbed wire. It is comprised of almost 0.7 square miles (1.8 square km) of land, about 6 miles (10 km) of roadway, and 31 buildings that make up a fake town. There is a mock airport and fake Air Force One and Marine One, the president's airplane and helicopter. Trainees take part in training scenarios at the facility, where they learn how to behave in different incidents.

Trainees learn how to protect the president in a fake Air Force One, so that they will be ready to take action in the real thing.

Secret Scenarios

The fake town allows trainees to take part in pretend missions that feel like real life. They rehearse using motorcades and simulated attacks in a tightly controlled environment. The town has high windows, from where an agent pretending to be a sniper can fire shots, and buildings where recruits can practice clearing innocent people. On the city streets, they learn driving skills such as evasive maneuvers, high-speed cornering, and precision driving, which could help them get the president to safety. In some scenarios, agents dress as terrorists or famous leaders to put trainees through their paces. At other times, trainees take turns rehearsing with each other, for example, in how to subdue or disarm an attacker or how to arrest a suspect who is holed up in a busy bar where there are lots of innocent people who could get hurt.

A Replica White House?

The training center has small mock-ups of White House rooms that are not to scale and makeshift White House fences built on a parking lot. However, the U.S. Secret Service would like to build a replica of the White House, with details such as the bushes and fountains, to help agents train to protect the president. It would be an actual copy of the facade of the White House residence, the East and West Wings, guard booths, and the surrounding grounds and roads.

Trainee agents practice shooting at a shooting range.

You Are Hired!

Secret Service training is long and tough, and it is designed to put the future agents and officers under intense pressure. Only the very best recruits make it to the end and pass the exams and tests they have to undergo as training. As well as the 2,000 technical, professional, and administrative support personnel, the Secret Service employs approximately 3,200 special agents and 1,300 Uniformed Division officers. Once they are hired, new Secret Service special agents and officers swear an oath to their country. Then, they start work.

An Agent's Career Path

Agents spend their first six to eight years working at a field office somewhere in the United States. After this, they usually transfer to a protective detail where they will stay for three to five years. Following their protective assignment, many agents return to the field, transfer to a headquarters office, a training office, or to another Washington, D.C.-based assignment. At some point during their career, agents may have a chance to work overseas in one of the agency's international field offices. There, they will need to learn the language spoken by their colleagues, so that they can work alongside them.

President Barack Obama speaks to proud Secret Service Uniformed Division officers in front of the White House.

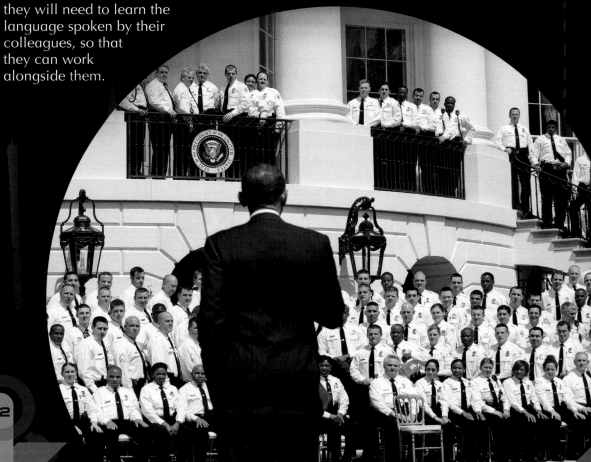

Training for Life

Secret Service agents continue to train throughout their careers. They have regular firearms and emergency medicine refresher courses. Those who work in protection details involving Secret Service protectees regularly do crisis training scenarios at the training center to improve their ability to respond to a variety of emergency situations. New agents should not expect life to get any easier. The training never stops, and each day, protecting the president and others or investigating crimes bring their own challenges and dangers.

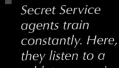

Secret Service agents train constantly. Here, they listen to a tabletop exercise in preparation for a presidential inauguration.

The Secret Service Oath

"I, [name], do solemnly swear (or affirm) that I will support and defend the Constitution of the United States against all enemies, foreign and domestic; that I will bear true faith and allegiance to the same; that I take this obligation freely, without any mental reservation or purpose of evasion; and that I will well and faithfully discharge the duties of the office on which I am about to enter. So help me God."

A COVERT CAREER WITH THE SECRET SERVICE

Would you like a career with the Secret Service? Following these steps will set you on your path.

At School

It is good to study hard in all subjects in school to learn the variety of skills that Secret Service agents use. These include science, computer science, law and government, arithmetic, reading comprehension, writing, foreign languages, and public speaking.

Background Checks

Everyone who applies to join the Secret Service undergoes a background investigation to check if, for example, they have ever taken illegal drugs, been in financial trouble, or have a police record.

At College

Most applicants have a four-year college degree or a combination of education and criminal investigative experience.

Physical Fitness

Secret Service agents must be physically fit and have to pass a series of rigorous physical and medical tests as part of the application and training process.

Age Requirements

When they apply for a job, Secret Service candidates must be at least 21 years old and younger than 37 at the time of appointment.

Successful Applicants

Criminal Investigator Training Program (CITP): New trainees do a 56-day course that includes lectures, laboratory activities, practical exercises, and written exams in such areas as criminal law and investigative techniques. They learn such skills as how to interview witnesses, how to do surveillance and undercover operations, how to write and execute search and arrest warrants, write a criminal complaint, and give evidence in a courtroom hearing.

Special Agent Training Course: After CITP, trainees complete a 17-week course at the James J. Rowley Training Center, learning skills needed for investigation and protection missions. These include skills such as using firearms, making arrests, combating counterfeiting, investigating potential threats, surveillance, how to do security surveys, and emergency first aid.

Becoming a Secret Service Agent: When trainees become Secret Service agents, they swear an oath to support and defend the Constitution of the United States against all enemies. They begin working immediately in a Secret Service field office somewhere in the United States.

GLOSSARY

aerobic Describes energetic physical exercises that make people breathe harder than usual.

background checks Investigations into a person's past activities—including checks to find out if they have been involved in any crimes.

Constitution The U.S. system of laws that formally states people's rights and duties.

counterfeit An exact copy of something valuable, made with the intention to deceive or defraud.

credentials Evidence that proves a person does have the qualifications or job that they say they have.

cybercrime Criminal activities carried out by means of computers or the Internet.

database A collection of information held on a computer that is organized so that it can be easily accessed, managed, and updated.

federal To do with central government.

field offices Offices away from an organization's main office that are part of the main operation.

forensics Scientific tests or techniques used in connection with the detection of crime.

GPS The acronym for Global Positioning System, a satellite-based navigation system.

identity theft Stealing someone else's personal information in order to obtain money or credit.

intelligence Information that concerns a criminal, an enemy, or a possible enemy.

latent fingerprints Fingerprints made of the sweat and oil on the skin's surface.

magnetometers Machines that can be used as metal detectors.

money laundering The methods criminals use to make it appear as if money obtained from criminal activity was made legally.

oath A solemn promise.

protectees People who are protected.

psychology The study of the human mind and how it makes people behave as they do.

satellite A machine placed in orbit around the earth to collect information or for communication.

scenarios Expected or supposed situations or sequences of events.

security clearance Official permission for someone to see classified information.

sniper A person who shoots from a hiding place, especially accurately and at long range.

summits Meetings between heads of government.

surveillance Close and careful observation of someone or something to gather intelligence.

terrorism The unlawful use of violence and threat to force a government or country to do what the terrorists want.

FOR MORE INFORMATION

BOOKS

Colich, Abby. *U.S. Federal Agents: Secret Service Agents*.
North Mankato, MN: Capstone Press, 2018.

Lassieur, Allison. *Cyber Spies and Secret Agents of Modern Times*.
North Mankato, MN: Compass Point Books, 2017.

Roberts, Jack L. *The Story of the U.S. Secret Service*. North Charleston,
SC: CreateSpace Independent Publishing, 2017.

Shea, Therese. *Federal Forces: Careers As Federal Agents: A Career As a
Secret Service Agent*. New York, NY: PowerKids Press, 2015.

WEBSITES

Find out why the Secret Service protects the president's children at:
people.howstuffworks.com/why-does-the-secret-service-protect-a-
presidents-adult-children.htm

Read more about Secret Service careers at:
www.secretservice.gov/join/careers

The official Secret Service website has lots of information at:
www.secretservice.gov

This Encyclopedia Britannica entry has lots of dates and facts
about the Secret Service:
www.britannica.com/topic/US-Secret-Service

INDEX